structures dating from Roman days right up to the present time.

Medieval and Tudor buildings are as much a part of Exeter's workaday fabric as a supermarket or the bus station. One of the city's oldest churches – the tiny St Pancras, dating from the 12th century at the latest – stands in the precincts of a central shopping mall, and local councillors meet in the Guildhall, said to be Britain's oldest municipal building, first mentioned in a deed of 1160.

Exeter Historic Quayside, on the River Exe, brings reminders of the city's maritime past, when bales of woollen cloth were manhandled aboard sailing ships to be traded in Europe, the Mediterranean and the Americas for timber, iron ore, sugar, tobacco and wines.

Above all in this city of 100,000 people is the Cathedral Church of St Peter, whose distinctive twin towers have witnessed Exeter's progress from the days of the Normans to the start of the third millennium.

BELOW **A sight of the magnificent west front of St Peter's Cathedral, dated 1329, with its outstanding stone image screen, is one of the highlights of a trip to Exeter.**

History

Founded by the Romans around AD 50, Exeter is one of the oldest towns in Britain. There may have been a settlement here earlier – humans had certainly been living in the Exe Valley and other parts of Devon for centuries – but once the Romans recognized its strategic importance, they lost no time in setting up a garrison on the hilly spur overlooking a point where the River Exe could easily be crossed.

Although evidence has been unearthed of military camps north and south of Dartmoor and even in Cornwall, Exeter – Isca Dumnoniorum, to the Romans –

effectively marked the westward extent of the Roman Empire. The local Celts, the Dumnonii, did not welcome the invaders and there were frequent skirmishes, so earth fortifications were built around the garrison. Work on a massive red-stone wall, large parts of which remain, finished around AD 200.

Supplies to the frontier settlement came from the east by land, along what is now the A30, and by water, on vessels navigating the River Exe to the site of present-day Topsham. Trading principally in agriculture, metal products and pottery, Roman Isca flourished.

A clue to the lifestyle enjoyed by the colonists came to light in 1971

BELOW **Decorative Tudor frieze from the 11th-century St Nicholas Priory.**

RIGHT **Athelstan's Tower, named after Alfred the Great's grandson, who was crowned king of England in 925, was not built until the 12th century. It can be seen in Rougemont Gardens.**

BELOW **The Cathedral's Norman twin towers provide an inspiring view from the city's approaches. Most of the rest of the building dates from the 14th century.**

when a large, ornate bath-house, dating from about AD 60, was uncovered during demolition of the Church of St Mary Major. Unfortunately there were no funds available to preserve the remains, which now lie buried beneath the grass opposite the west front of the Cathedral.

Like other places in Britain, Exeter went into decline after the Roman legions were withdrawn to fight off barbarian attacks in Gaul and Italy. In 680 Exeter became part of the Kingdom of Wessex and the Christian Saxons built a monastery on the site of the Roman forum.

Important under the Anglo-Saxons, Exeter became a target for the Danes, who occupied the town twice – in 876, when they were sent packing by Alfred the Great, and 1003. In 1050 Edward the Confessor transferred the bishopric from Crediton to Exeter and the monastery church in the town centre became a cathedral.

After the Norman invasion and the Battle of Hastings, Glytha, mother of the defeated King Harold, fled with her daughter to Exeter, and in 1068, after being besieged for 18 days by an army headed by William the Conqueror, the city surrendered.

Asserting his supremacy over defiant Devonians, William built Rougemont Castle at the highest point of the city's walls. Now containing Exeter Crown Court, the castle still represents the State's authority.

The Conqueror's nephew, Bishop William Warelwast, authorized the building of a new cathedral, completed in 1160. Its twin towers form the most dominant external feature of the structure we see today.

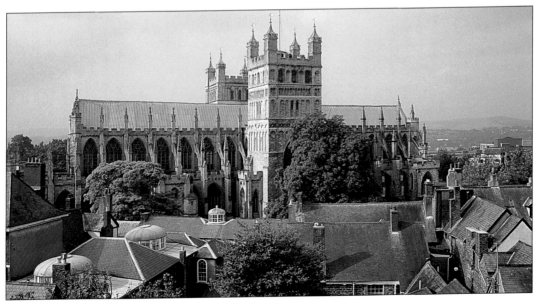

RIGHT
Hogenburg's map of Exeter, issued in 1587, shows the complete city wall before traffic requirements in later years led to the demolition of parts of it. This is one of the earliest views of an English town.

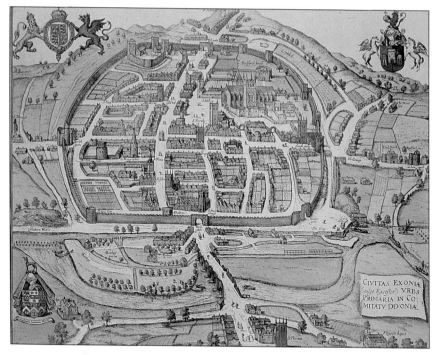

Sir Thomas Bodley.

The founder of Oxford's Bodleian Library, Sir Thomas Bodley, was born in Exeter in 1545. A brilliant scholar, he took a BA degree at Oxford at the age of 18 and a year later was admitted a Fellow of Merton College. Having studied Greek and Hebrew, he went on to become proficient in several other languages, particularly French, Italian and Spanish, and undertook numerous important diplomatic commissions.

The Normans' Rougemont Castle was put to the test when Exeter suffered its third siege – this time in the mid-12th century during the strife-ridden reign of the Conqueror's grandson, Stephen, who claimed the throne after William's son, Henry I, died in 1135.

In 1260 the cathedral built by William Warelwast was demolished, except for the two towers which were incorporated into the new building, completed in 1394.

Exeter once more began to flourish as a centre of trade, with Topsham again assuming the role of entrepôt, as it had during Roman times. Transhipped cargoes could be taken upstream by small craft, but Exeter was cut off from the sea for nearly 280 years after the Countess of Devon spitefully built a weir across the River Exe around 1285.

During the 13th and 14th centuries the city's piped domestic water supply, believed to date from the late 12th century, was considerably extended – a rare luxury for medieval

communities – and some of the tunnels that carried the system form the Underground Passages toured by visitors today.

The city remained loyal to Henry VII when Perkin Warbeck, claiming to be Richard, the younger son of Edward IV and one of the ill-fated Princes in the Tower, attempted to invade England after landing in Cornwall in 1497. Henry gratefully presented the city with a Sword of State and a Cap of Maintenance, both still carried in mayoral processions.

Despite difficulties created by the abolition of the monasteries, the 16th century saw Exeter becoming more affluent as the woollen cloth trade expanded. The obstruction caused by the Countess of Devon's weir was overcome by the building of England's first pound-lock canal in 1564–6, and the city became an important port.

Turmoil, however, continued. The city became involved in the violent Prayer Book Rebellion of 1549 when there was a big movement against the

new English Protestant prayer book. The rebellion was quashed in a bloody battle at Clyst St Mary, about 4 miles (6km) east of Exeter.

During the Civil War, in which the city supported first one side then the other, Exeter was besieged twice – in 1643 and 1645–6.

Further violence was experienced during World War II, when heavy bombing in 1942 destroyed a large part of the city, including the library, the lower market and six churches. The Cathedral suffered extensive damage. Since the war, however, there has been considerable restoration and rebuilding. The University of Exeter, which began as the University College of the South-West in 1922, has matched the city's post-war development and with the Northcott Theatre on campus makes a considerable contribution to Exeter's amenities. The university can be found on the city's northern edge, off New North Road.

Another of Exeter's famous sons was Nicholas Hilliard, the first English painter of miniatures, who was born in the city in 1537. The son of a high sheriff of Devon, he was apprenticed to a jeweller and goldsmith, and became an accomplished miniaturist while still in his teens. His most renowned miniatures are portraits of Mary Queen of Scots and Elizabeth I. He died in 1619.

BELOW **The Exeter Puzzle Jug (*c.* AD 1300), discovered in South Street in 1899, was imported from western France.**

ABOVE **The building of Exeter University began in 1925; full university status came 30 years later.**

LEFT **The Memorial Fountain in Princesshay was erected in 1992, the 50th anniversary of the Blitz that destroyed much of the city centre.**

The Cathedral

Silhouetted against the sky and visible for miles along the approaches to the city, the north and south towers of Exeter Cathedral – St Paul's and St John's Towers respectively – have stood proud for nearly nine centuries.

RIGHT St Paul's Tower, on the Cathedral's north side, houses the 1484 Peter bell.

BELOW Detail from the uppermost of the three rows of sculpted figures on the magnificent west front of Exeter Cathedral.

William the Conqueror's nephew, William Warelwast, the third Bishop of Exeter (served from 1107 to 1137), started building the Cathedral around 1110 to replace a monastery church that had occupied the site for the previous 70 years. The monastery church had been elevated to cathedral status when Edward the Confessor transferred the see of Crediton to Exeter in 1050.

Warelwast's 130ft (40m) Norman towers are the only original parts of the Cathedral. The rest was demolished around 1260, the present Cathedral being built between that date and the late 1300s.

Impressive though the towers are, it is the magnificently ornate west front, dating from 1329, that is perhaps St Peter's Cathedral's leading claim to fame.

The building has a number of features that are greatly admired by ecclesiastical historians and lay people alike. Among these are the

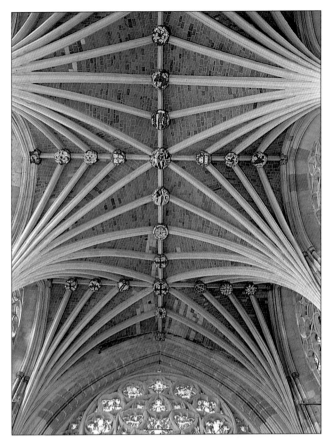

ABOVE An angel gazes from the rows of stone figures on the west front.

ABOVE The rib-vaulting in the nave is one of the Cathedral's most splendid features.

RIGHT One of the coloured bosses depicts the murder of Archbishop Thomas Becket.

wealth of 14th-century stained glass, the rib-vaulting in the nave, the detailed bosses, the minstrels' gallery, the 15th-century clock in the north transept, the 49 misericords (it is believed that these form the only complete set in England) and the bishop's lofty throne.

A tour of the Cathedral recalls historical events of more than eight

centuries, from the murder of Thomas Becket in 1170 to the heavy bombing of Exeter during World War II.

Visitors enter by the west door, on the left-hand side of the west front as you face it, and are requested to contribute to the cost of the constant work needed to keep the fabric in good repair.

But before going inside, most people want to spend a few minutes – or considerably longer – feasting their eyes on the west front. Here the stone image screen presents three rows of sculpted figures, which include Jesus Christ, William the Conqueror, King Athelstan, Edward the Confessor and Richard II.

The top tier shows 28 ecclesiastical figures, with Christ just off centre, fifteenth from the left. In the middle row are seated kings, including William the Conqueror. The bottom tier is occupied by angels, some of them playing musical instruments. The key identifying all the figures apparently no longer exists.

Much of the west front's screen was originated during the incumbency of Bishop John Grandisson, who served between 1327 and 1369 and is buried in a small chapel within the thickness of the screen. Some figures were repaired or replaced in the 19th and 20th centuries.

Inside, the nave is a heart-lifting sight, particularly when shafts of evening sunlight through the stained glass of the great west window emphasize the colour of the Purbeck marble pillars and adjacent stonework.

The astonishing vault, 68ft (21m) above the nave floor, is said to be the longest unbroken stretch of Gothic vaulting in the world. Along its central spine and cross-members are bosses,

or carved and coloured circular plaques; some are decorative designs, some depict biblical or historical scenes. One of the latter illustrates the murder of Archbishop Thomas Becket in Canterbury Cathedral.

The Cathedral authorities have provided a concave mirror set into a wheeled trolley, which visitors can push along the aisle to study the roof vaulting and bosses without ricking their necks.

The peal of 14 bells is housed in the south tower. Until Liverpool Cathedral usurped its position in recent years, it was claimed to be the world's heaviest peal. In the north tower is a 4-ton (4-tonne) bell donated by Bishop Peter Courtenay in 1484 and known as the Peter bell. This is the bell that resonantly strikes the hours for Exeter's citizens and visitors alike.

Twelve sculpted angels, each with a different 14th-century musical instrument, adorn the minstrels' gallery. The wind instrument that one

BELOW **The bishop's throne, carved with elaborate ornamentation from Devon oak and completed in 1312, is nearly 60ft (18m) high. It was constructed without nails, and is a particularly impressive example of early craftsmanship.**

BELOW **The 15th-century astrological clock in the north transept shows not only the hours but also the passage of the sun and moon around the earth.**

ABOVE Four of the twelve angel musicians in the minstrels' gallery.

BELOW The famous Exeter Elephant, one of the Cathedral misericords carved 650 years ago.

unfortunate angel is attempting to play was broken some centuries ago.

The elaborately carved bishop's throne, dating from 1312 and considered the finest in England, was the gift of Bishop Walter Stapledon, the founder of Exeter College, Oxford, who was murdered in 1326 by a mob in London because he was treasurer to the unpopular King Edward II.

The mid-13th-century misericords below each of the 49 choir stalls have been preserved and reincorporated whenever restoration work has been carried out. All are highly imaginative in design, but the most famous is the Exeter Elephant. It was carved by someone who had never seen an elephant, and he made a very good job of it except for the feet, which resemble protruding hooves.

Stained glass, tablets and brass plaques around the Cathedral commemorate events in many parts of the world in which West Country people took part. Wars and conflicts down the years in Europe, South Africa and other countries have taken their toll.

The beautiful east window dates from about 1390, the period around which much of the Cathedral's stained glass originated.

RIGHT Floodlit after dark, the Cathedral's west front provides a dramatic aspect for evening strollers.

RIGHT The west window glass is modern, but like its 1904 predecessor it features important figures from the Cathedral's history.

There are tombs and effigies of past bishops of Exeter and other dignitaries in a variety of styles. In addition to the tomb of Bishop Bronescombe (see panel opposite), look for the lavishly decorated resting place of Bishop Hugh Oldham, who served from 1504 to 1519. He was founder of Manchester Grammar School and co-founder of Corpus Christi College, Oxford.

The high altar has not been backed by a reredos since 1939, but the highly regarded 'Exeter pillar' with its 16 shafts now provides a splendid backdrop. Much of the stained glass was extensively damaged in World War II. It was in May 1942 that Exeter was targeted by enemy bombers, and the Cathedral suffered, though not as severely as some other parts of the

Bishop Walter Bronescombe, who served from 1257 to 1280, personally selected the site for his richly ornate tomb in the Cathedral. His effigy, in black basalt with original colouring intact, is considered one of the finest in the country. The tomb's canopy and base are 15th century. During his incumbency, Bishop Bronescombe instigated a major rebuilding of the Cathedral.

city. Some believe the bombing was a reprisal for the allied attack on Lübeck.

The ancient stained glass, with major works from the Victorian and Edwardian eras, was a predictable casualty. Some experts consider the replacements, produced between the late 1940s and mid-1950s, are less worthy, but the Christopher Webb glass commemorating the 1942 air raid is interesting.

Guidebooks to the Cathedral, as well as souvenirs and gifts, can be bought at the Cathedral shop. Coffees, lunches and teas are served in the refectory between 10am and 5pm, Monday to Saturday. Permits to take photographs in the Cathedral can be bought for 50p at the information desk. Between April and October guided tours are available from Monday to Friday at 11am and 2.30pm, and 11am on Saturday, subject to Cathedral commitments.

During term the Cathedral Choir usually sings daily except Wednesday. The Cathedral Voluntary Choir and visiting choirs sing during vacations.

ABOVE **The ornate choir screen dates from the 14th century, although its recently restored biblical paintings are early 17th-century.**

RIGHT **Lady Dodderidge, wife of the Solicitor-General, and her macabre companion. She died in 1614.**

Cathedral Close

A statue on
Cathedral Green
commemorates
Richard Hooker,
a 16th-century
theologian and
writer who was
born at
Heavitree,
Exeter, around
1553. He was an
unprepossessing
figure – shy and
short-sighted
with a badly
pimpled face –
but his sermons
and writings
were acclaimed
by the thinkers
of his day.

Peace and a strong sense of history
pervade Cathedral Close, the triangle
of grass and trees surrounded by fine
buildings dating from the 14th century.

The **Ship Inn**, in narrow Martin's
Lane, is said to have been one of Sir
Francis Drake's favourite taverns.
Words attributed to him appear on a
board outside the inn: 'Next to my
own ship I do most love that old Ship
in Exon, a tavern in Fish Street, as the
people call it, or as the clergy will
have it, St Martin's Lane.'

Sir Francis, Sir Walter Raleigh and
possibly other famous Elizabethan
figures – Frobisher, Greville, Hawkins

– are believed to have met at nearby
Mol's Coffee House, a much
photographed timber-framed house
dated 1596. Its Dutch-style gable was
added in the mid-1880s. It may have
been during their meetings at Mol's
that Drake and his colleagues planned
how to foil the Spanish Armada.

Mol's is now used as a commercial
property. Some people think it was
never a coffee house in the modern
sense, but was probably more like a
gentlemen's club. A frieze above the
late-Elizabethan panelling in a first-
floor room bears 46 coats of arms,
including those of Raleigh and Drake.

East of the Cathedral, an entrance
to Cathedral Close runs beneath an
attractive **cast-iron footbridge** that
spans a 19ft (6m) break in the city
wall. The bridge bears the date 1814

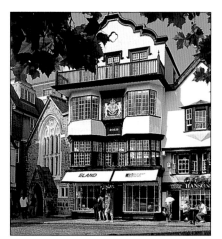

RIGHT Mol's Coffee
House, an Exeter
landmark for four
centuries.

ABOVE The sign of the Ship Inn,
reputedly one of Drake's favourite
taverns and still a popular hostelry.

RIGHT Some of
the coats of arms
in Mol's Coffee
House, among
which are Drake's
and Raleigh's.

A regular at Exeter's Ship Inn, the Devon-born buccaneer and explorer Sir Francis Drake inherited his first ship from the master to whom he had been apprenticed. He was the first English navigator to sail around the world (1577–80) and was a favourite of Elizabeth I for his actions against the Spaniards, especially for routing the Armada off Plymouth in 1588.

BELOW AND RIGHT The 15th-century official residence of the Bishop of Crediton is reached via an intricately carved oak doorway.

and the name of the mayor of the time, Burnet Patch.

A little further on are several houses dating from the 15th century. A magnificent and imposing arched doorway leads to nos. 10 and 11 Cathedral Close, the official residence of the Bishop of Crediton. The archway has a stone surround and the massive oak door is intricately carved.

Another interesting property, now converted to commercial premises, is **Annivellars' Refectory**, built in the early 15th century. Annivellars were chantry priests who said masses for the souls of their benefactors on the

ABOVE The 1814 cast-iron footbridge, erected by Mayor Burnet Patch, spans a break in the city wall.

anniversaries of their deaths.

The former town house of the Courtenay family, Earls of Devon, at **7 Cathedral Yard**, survived the Blitz and became the home of the Devon and Exeter Institute, an organization for the promotion of science, literature and the arts.

A walk in Exeter

This walk starts in the city centre, beside a section of the old Roman wall. It takes in Exeter's major historic and architectural sites, including the quayside on the River Exe, and ends with the splendour of St Peter's Cathedral. The full walk takes about 1½ hours, but may be shortened.

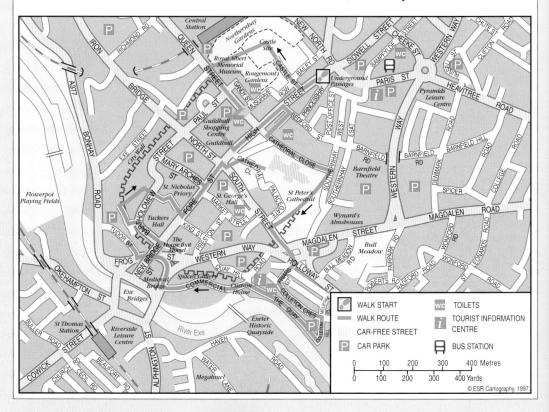

The walk starts at the northern end of Princesshay at the medieval north-east angle tower of the **old city wall** (page 4), (*right*). A line of crazy paving marks the wall's course towards the site of the East Gate, indicated by a plaque at High Street.

Cross High Street, where the entrance to the **Underground Passages** (page 20) is next to Boots the Chemist, and continue to the left, turning right into Castle Street, and up to the

entrance to **Rougemont Gardens**. On the right is a Norman gatehouse, on the left a discovery centre for school groups.

Continue through the gardens to the city wall, where a short tunnel leads into **Northernhay Gardens**. From here, walk downhill to Queen Street and turn left, passing the **Royal Albert Memorial Museum** (page 25). The first turning to the left after the museum leads into colourful **Gandy Street** (*right*), which dates from the Middle Ages.

Continue down Queen Street. On the right is the neo-classical façade of the Victorian Higher Market (page 25), now the entrance to the **Guildhall Shopping Centre**.

In the shopping centre, turn left at **St Pancras Church** (page 23), then right into Waterbeer Street and left again into **Parliament Street**, said to be the narrowest in the world – it is just 45in wide (114cm) at most.

At the end of the alley, turn left along High Street, where the most striking building is the ornate medieval **Guildhall** (page 21), (*above*).

Crossing to the right-hand side, continue along High Street and turn right under the archway at St Stephen's Bow to the ruined **St Catherine's Almshouses** (page 18) in

Catherine Street, where a left turn leads to **Cathedral Close** (pages 14–15, 18–19), (*left*), passing **St Martin's Church** (page 18), **Mol's Coffee House** (page 14) and Martin's Lane, home to the **Ship Inn** (page 14).

Continue along Cathedral Close, under the **cast-iron bridge** (pages 14–15) into Southernhay West and turn right. At the rear of nos. 1–10 Southernhay West, walk down the steps, pass the Forte Crest Hotel and follow the city wall to South Street.

Cross South Street and Western Way into Holloway Street, then head down Friars' Gate, turning left into **Colleton Crescent** (page 24), which has some fine Georgian buildings. Go down Colleton Hill to **The Quay** (pages 26–7), (*right*),

and turn right, passing the **Custom House** (*right*) and heading along Commercial Road.

At the end of Commercial Road, a subway leads to the ruins of **St Edmund's Church** and the **medieval bridge** (page 27).

From the second subway head along New Bridge Street, diverting left into Tudor Street to see **Tudor House**, dated *c.* 1660 (*left*), then right into West Street to examine the **House that Moved** (page 22), **Stepcote Hill** (page 22) and **St Mary Steps Church** (page 23).

Return along West Street and cross Fore Street, which at this end contains the 15th-century **Tuckers Hall** (page 22), into Bartholomew Street West and on to Bartholomew Terrace, where a number of pleasant 18th- and 19th-century buildings follow the course of the city wall. At the end of the terrace, turn right and continue to The Mint, where **St Nicholas Priory** (pages 20–21) was founded in 1087.

At Fore Street turn left, diverting into Mary Arches Street to see **St Mary Arches Church**, (*above*), before crossing South Street. After **St Petrock's Church** (page 19), bear right into Cathedral Close for a view of the magnificent west front of **St Peter's Cathedral** (pages 8–13).

RIGHT **In stark contrast to the nearby busy High Street are the desolate ruins of St Catherine's Chapel and Almshouses, dating from the mid-15th century. Today they serve as a reminder of the 1942 Blitz to which the buildings succumbed.**

In a corner of the Cathedral Close is **St Martin's Church**, dedicated to St Martin of Tours, patron saint of beggars. It was consecrated in 1065 – making it one of the city's oldest churches – and partially rebuilt in the 15th century. The stonework around the windows is of Beer stone, quarried at Beer in East Devon and extensively used in parts of the Cathedral itself.

Also of special interest in St Martin's are the chancel arch, the oak wagon roof, the altar rails and the font.

In Catherine Street the walls of **St Catherine's Chapel**, from 1458, and **St Catherine's Almshouses**, founded in 1450, stand evocatively in ruins. The buildings were the victim of aerial bombardment in World War II and their shells are preserved as a reminder of the Blitz. When the rubble was cleared from Catherine Street, a Roman tessellated pavement was revealed beneath.

Behind the Cathedral Chapter House, at the south-east corner of the

RIGHT St Martin's Church originally dates from 1065, making it one of the oldest in Exeter.

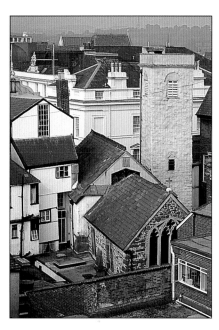

Cathedral, **St Petrock's**. This saint was known as the Apostle of the West. He entered a monastery as a young man and later spent time in Rome and Jerusalem, as well as Ireland and the West of England.

The north-west tower of St Petrock's Church has a small octagonal turret dated 1736. Alterations were made to the church in the early 1400s and further enlargements took place between then and the 1820s. The original chancel, facing east, has been screened off since a new chancel, facing south, was added in 1881. This has had the effect of turning around the whole direction of the church; as a result, the interior is regarded as something of a curiosity.

Cathedral, is the **Bishop's Palace**. The Cathedral School is also nearby.

Near the Cathedral's west front is the **Devon War Memorial**, a simple structure of granite designed by Sir Edwin Lutyens.

BELOW The Royal Clarence Hotel, Cathedral Yard, built in the 1760s as assembly rooms. Over the years it has received such luminaries as the Duchess of Clarence (later Queen Adelaide), Lord Nelson and Tsar Nicholas I.

In medieval days there were several entrances to the Close. An enclosing wall was built in the late 13th century after violent attacks on the clergy during the hours of darkness. One Cathedral official was murdered in 1285.

One of the medieval entrances was near another church close to the

ABOVE The walls inside St Petrock's Church are hung with a sequence of sombre memorials dating from the 17th and 18th centuries.

Medieval and Tudor buildings

RIGHT A modern monastic-style window installed in the Benedictine St Nicholas Priory after restoration work by Exeter Corporation.

Exeter's city wall, built by the Romans around AD 200, has some gaps in it today because of the demands of city planning over the years. But much of it survives, and is in good repair. Within it are a number of remarkably well-preserved buildings dating from medieval and Tudor times. The Cathedral (pages 8–13) is just one example.

Most visitors are fascinated by the **Underground Passages**, believed to be the only medieval subterranean waterways open to the public in the country. Guided tours can be taken of the 14th- and 15th-century tunnels along which fresh water flowed from springs outside the walls, providing the local population with the luxury of a constant supply.

At The Mint, off Fore Street, close to the city centre, is **St Nicholas Priory**. A monastery with its own church, it was built by monks and dedicated to St Nicholas in 1087. The monks had been despatched from Battle Abbey, in Sussex, by William the Conqueror in 1068 to administer St Olave's Church in Exeter.

RIGHT Richly ornamented period furniture, such as this chest, can be seen in St Nicholas Priory, built by Benedictine monks in the 11th century and converted to private residential use during Elizabethan times.

ABOVE **The late 16th-century dark oak door to the main hall of the Guildhall has much decorative carving.**

ABOVE **Locally quarried stone was used in the building of Exeter's cherished Guildhall and local carpenters were responsible for the timber roof. The present building, dating from the 1590s, replaced a 12th-century meeting place at the site. Four granite pillars support the front of the structure.**

The original priory was extended in the 12th and 13th centuries, and much of it was demolished at the time of the dissolution of smaller monasteries by Henry VIII in 1536.

About a quarter of the original priory remains. From Elizabethan times until the early 1900s it was used as residences. In 1913 Exeter Corporation bought it and restored its monastic style.

The cloister entrance, the Undercroft, where beer and provisions were stored (built around 1100), and a first-floor bed chamber and the Great Hall – both from the 15th century, with superb arch-braced timber roof – are open to the public.

Exeter is justly proud of its **Guildhall**, situated in the High Street, one of the oldest municipal buildings in the country still in use today. The present building dates from the 14th century, and a previous meeting place is known to have existed on the site in 1160.

The present portico, with four granite pillars supporting the Mayor's Parlour, was built in the 1590s at a cost, according to records that survive, of £782. The five original windows of the Mayor's Parlour and the late 15th-century timber roof of the Guildhall are of architectural importance.

Charles Dickens, who spent more than three years in the Exeter area in the 1830s, had associations with the **Turk's Head**, next to the Guildhall. Part of the old timbered inn was used as a jail for a time, and the name is said to derive from the execution of a Turkish prisoner.

an attic, the richly timbered house was prepared for a short journey on rollers into West Street, where it looks perfectly at home. It is now known as **the House that Moved**.

Stepcote Hill, off West Street, is steep and narrow, looking picturesque and quaint to modern eyes, but it was the main western route into the city from medieval times until 200 years ago. Pedestrians now walk the 100 steps on either side of the strip of cobblestones once used by pack horses.

BELOW **Stepcote Hill, a narrow, cobblestoned pack-horse track flanked by 100 steps, was once the main western route into Exeter.**

ABOVE **A Tudor timber-framed house in the city has been known as the House that Moved since 1961, when it was transported on rollers 75yd (70m) from its original site.**

RIGHT **Tiny St Pancras Church, possibly partly pre-Norman, is encountered unexpectedly in the Guildhall Shopping Centre.**

The south-western end of High Street becomes Fore Street (and then New Bridge Street). In Fore Street is the **Tuckers Hall**, a substantial 1471 building with Jacobean panelling and a Victorian façade. Exeter's prosperity was at one time based on woollen cloth, and the Tuckers Hall became the meeting place of the Guild of Weavers, Fullers and Shearmen. Fullers, or tuckers, were the people whose job it was to remove the grease from sheep's wool.

Moving house took on a whole new meaning in 1961 when major roadworks threatened the future of an early 15th-century building, which it was felt should be saved. Only one room wide but with three floors and

The **White Hart Hotel** in South Street, a former coaching inn, originated in the 15th century as a resting house for monks. During restoration work in 1955 an early English fireplace, now incorporated into the bar, was discovered and is considered one of the finest of its type in the West Country.

Wynard's Almshouses in Magdalen Street date from 1436. A courtyard, with the quarters of 12 pensioners on three sides and a chapel on the fourth, is open in the daytime. The south-west corner provides a panoramic view of the city.

ABOVE **In the 15th century travellers and their horses found rest and sustenance at the White Hart Hotel; today, rooms and refreshment are still available – but now only for people.**

Close by is **St Mary Steps Church**, founded in the 12th century and rebuilt in the 15th. Its 1620s clock has three figures – perhaps Henry VIII and two attendants – which go into action when the hour strikes.

Exeter is one of those compact, walk-around cities where the first-time visitor is repeatedly enchanted by historic sights. Such a surprise is found in a clearing in the modern Guildhall Shopping Centre, namely the venerable church of **St Pancras**, only 16ft (5m) wide and less than 50ft (15m) long. It is one of the oldest churches in Exeter, and some believe the font to be pre-Norman.

BELOW **A monogrammed floor tile in the wellhead at Wynard's Almshouses.**

RIGHT **Wynard's Almshouses, built by William Wynard in 1436, underwent considerable restoration in the 19th century. The houses, together with Trinity Chapel, surround a cobbled courtyard.**

Georgian and Victorian buildings

ABOVE A fine Georgian terrace in Southernhay. Many buildings of the period were lost in the bombardment of 1942.

Exeter has a wealth of Georgian buildings that survived the bombings of World War II. Built by the merchants who prospered in the city during the late 18th and early 19th centuries, many are to be found in and around the city centre, most of them now used as offices. **Barnfield Crescent**, off Barnfield Road, an elegantly curved four-storey terrace, was built in 1805 and now houses County Council and private offices.

The fine terraced houses in **Southernhay West** are a testament to those Industrial Revolution entrepreneurs who had not only the wisdom to put their money into property, but also the grace to make it an expression of good taste.

The original buildings of the **Royal Devon and Exeter Hospital** stand at the southern end of Southernhay East. The hospital opened in 1741, one of England's first provincial hospitals. Nearby is **Trinity Green**, the site of a graveyard where many victims of a cholera epidemic that struck in 1832 were buried.

Colleton Crescent, above and running parallel with The Quay, is another area of fine Georgian buildings – this time with the bonus of a splendid view across the River Exe to the Haldon Hills.

One of the city's most prominent Georgian buildings is the **Royal**

RIGHT Colleton Crescent's magnificent swathe of Georgian houses overlooks the river and provides a fine view from The Quay below.

LEFT Rougemont House (1774), built by John Patch, on land leased from the Duchy of Cornwall.

ABOVE The Royal Clarence is said to be the first establishment in England to have been called a hotel.

Clarence Hotel in Cathedral Yard. It was opened in 1769 by a Frenchman who simply called it The Hotel, the first time the term had been applied to overnight lodgings in England. Its present name honours the Duchess of Clarence, later Queen Adelaide, who twice stayed at the hotel.

Back at the top of the town, **Rougemont House**, standing at the entrance to Rougemont Gardens, was built in 1774 and enlarged by a wealthy wool merchant in 1787. Its gardens became a public park in 1912. Today the house serves as a discovery centre for school groups.

Victorian Exeter is to be found mainly in Queen Street, with the **Royal Albert Memorial Museum** forming the dominant feature. Opened in 1865, it is an extravagant statement in Venetian gothic style housing local history and fine art collections. A little further along Queen Street, on the opposite side, the Guildhall Shopping Centre is entered through the neo-classical façade of the former **Higher Market**, designed by Charles Fowler, the Devon architect also responsible for Covent Garden in London.

LEFT The façade of Marks and Spencer belies its recent origins having been reconstructed to harmonize with that of the adjacent neo-classical Higher Market.

The river and quay

Sixteenth-century engineers improved navigation on the River Exe by building a canal so that barges up to 16 tons (16.25 tonnes) could sail up to Exeter city wall. This enabled trade to expand and Exeter flourished as an international port exporting woollen cloth. It reached the peak of its prosperity in the 18th century.

Since the canal was completed in 1566, it has been extended, deepened and widened.

Today **Exeter Historic Quayside**, with its warehouses and wharf buildings, has become an inland waterway resort. Pubs, restaurants, cafés, craft and antique shops, pleasure boats, a cable ferry, historical buildings, and shops selling silks, hand-made crystal glass, and wine and beer home-brews make it a delightful place to stroll and browse.

The **Custom House** (1685), claimed to be the oldest in England, was the city's first major brick building and gives an indication of the level of importance maritime trade once held.

Almost every summer tourist enters **Quay House**, now a visitor centre, where an audio-visual presentation of 2,000 years of Exeter history is shown. Display boards outline the early days of quayside life, and souvenirs and cards are on sale.

ABOVE **Former bonded warehouses at The Quay were built into the cliff behind. In their heyday they stored a range of goods from silk to iron ore. Now some are part of the entertainment and tourist scene, with an interpretive centre in a converted 17th-century warehouse.**

RIGHT *Near The Quay, Exeter* (detail), by John White Abbott (1763–1851).

ABOVE **The Custom House, built in the 1680s, was the first major brick building erected in Exeter. It is believed the bricks were shipped from the Netherlands as ballast.**

The **canal** no longer carries commercial traffic and, sadly, the renowned Maritime Museum on the canal basin has closed, and its large collection of working boats has been dispersed. At the time of publication, however, Exeter City Council was inviting ideas for public and private initiatives to redevelop both the former Maritime Museum buildings and the canal basin.

The canal was constructed by John Trew and was the first in England to use pound locks. It is not difficult to imagine it in its heyday, when imports from Europe and the New World – including coal, timber, iron

ABOVE **The delightful Exeter Historic Quayside is now one of the city's major tourist attractions.**

ore, sugar, tobacco and wines – were unloaded here.

Today the canal is a recreational amenity. Groups of youngsters are put through their sailboard paces, and private pleasure boats arrive from the River Exe, their crews eager to stock up in the city centre a few minutes' walk away.

People can hire bicycles and canoes for towpath or waterborne exploring towards Topsham. Paddling party nights are popular, when canoeists are taken by a guide to a waterside pub, returning by moonlight.

A walk along Commercial Road from the Custom House leads to the substantial remains of an 800-year-old **bridge**, one of England's earliest long bridges at 600ft (183m), with at least 17 arches. The Exe now keeps to a narrower channel away from the bridge, which was replaced by a new structure in 1778.

BELOW **Butt's Ferry has operated at The Quay for 350 years.**

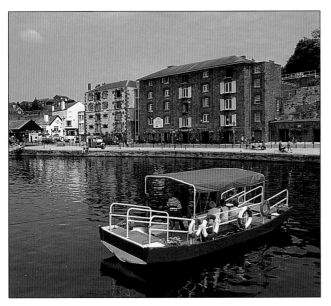

Excursions around Exeter

RIGHT **The 13th-century clapper bridge is a famous landmark at Postbridge. The nearby car park has a Dartmoor National Park information centre.**

As the major gateway to the South West Peninsula, Exeter is well placed for excursions to various country and coastal attractions – natural, historical, educational or simply pleasurable.

The area's best-known feature, **Dartmoor**, is reached by way of the A38 in little more than 10 miles (16km). Famous for its ponies and prison, Dartmoor National Park encompasses about 400sq miles (1,000sq km) of wild, rocky moorland and beautiful, rustic landscapes, about half of it some 1,000ft (300m) above sea-level.

BELOW **Castle Drogo, a National Trust property built by Sir Edwin Lutyens, overlooks the River Teign. Work started in 1910, and the huge castle was completed in 1930.**

Information on Dartmoor's history, legends, topography, animals and plants is available at the High Moorland Visitor Centre, Princeton. Leaflets and maps are distributed at centres in other parts of the park.

Castle Drogo, off the A382 near Drewsteignton, within the national park, is a granite castle built in medieval style between 1910 and 1930 by Sir Edwin Lutyens for a grocery magnate. It is now owned by the National Trust. **Powderham Castle**, about 8 miles (13km) south of the city, has been the home of the Courtenay family for more than 600 years and has magnificent halls and staterooms filled with lavish furnishings and works of art. The grounds include the Secret Garden, opened in 1997.

In the village of **Star Cross**, look out for the Atmospheric Railway, a pub named after one of Isambard Kingdom Brunel's few engineering

ABOVE
Powderham Castle, by the Exe Estuary. In summer trailer rides go to the Woodland Garden and Deer Park.

ABOVE RIGHT
Topsham's picturesque homes, its shore and the estuary, bright with fishing boats and pleasure craft, attract many visitors.

failures – a scheme involving special pistons and pumping stations to boost the power of locomotives pulling trains up the steep gradients on the Plymouth line.

Dawlish Warren Nature Reserve stands on a sandspit at the mouth of the River Exe. Rare flora flourishes here from spring to early summer, and at high tides – especially between August and April – it is a wonderful place for birdwatching.

North of Exeter, **Killerton House**, a National Trust property, was rebuilt in 1778 and contains a fine collection of costumes from the 18th century to the present day. The hillside gardens are a joy year round.

Fursdon House, near the ancient hillfort at Cadbury, is a Georgian mansion, though the Fursdon family has lived on the site since 1259. Displays relate to the family's history and there is also a costume collection.

Bickleigh village has a picturesque medieval castle and Devonshire's Centre, a complex of craft workshops, motor museum, narrow-gauge railway and farming exhibition based on an old mill.

Clyst St Mary, on Exeter's south-east fringe, is the home of **Crealy**, a large family pleasure park with a farm nursery, pets' corner, children's village and adventure grounds.

Topsham, an attractive maritime village at the head of the Exe Estuary, is noted for its antique shops and restaurants. Its museum, located in a merchant's house of the late 17th century, reflects the time when Topsham was a shipbuilding centre.

Exmouth's most unusual attraction is **A La Ronde**, a 16-sided house built in 1796. Now owned by the National Trust, it houses collections of items brought back from a European Grand Tour by the two unmarried cousins for whom it was built.

RIGHT **Killerton House (National Trust) has a hillside garden. A costume collection with pieces from the 18th century to the present day is exhibited in period rooms.**

BELOW **The 16-sided A La Ronde at Exmouth.**

Further information

Details are correct at the time of writing but may be changed.

Tourist Information Centre

Civic Centre, Paris Street (tel 01392 265700). Open Mon–Sat 9–5. Closed Sun.

Exeter Cathedral

Cathedral Green (tel 01392 214219). Open daily. Guided tours Apr–Oct (subject to Cathedral commitments) Mon–Fri 11 and 2.30, Sat 11. Donation requested.

Exeter Historic Quayside

Quay House Visitor Centre
46 The Quay (tel 01392 265213). Open Easter–Oct daily 10–5. Admission free.

Medieval and Tudor buildings

Underground Passages
High Street (entrance in Romangate Passage) (tel 01392 265887). Open Jul–Sep and school hols Mon–Sat 10–5.30 (last tour 4.45); rest of year Tue–Fri 2–5, Sat 10–5. Admission charge.

St Nicholas Priory
The Mint (tel 01392 265858). Open Easter–Oct Mon, Wed, Sat 3–4.30. Closed rest of year. Admission charge.

BELOW LEFT
The city motto, *Semper Fidelis*, seen here in stained glass in the Guildhall, means 'Always Faithful'.

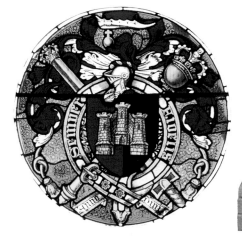

The Guildhall
High Street (tel 01392 265500). Open subject to civic requirements. Admission free.

Tuckers Hall
Fore Street (tel 01392 436244). Open Jun–Sep Tue, Thu, Fri 10.30–12.30; Oct–May Thu 10.30–12.30. Admission charge.

Festivals and events

Devon and County Show (May); Devon County Antiques Fair (Jun); Exeter Festival, Lammas Fair (Jul); Exeter Pageant, Medieval Fair (Aug).

BELOW Carole Vincent's 1989 sculpture in High Street was commissioned to commemorate the Year of the Pedestrian.